TEACH ON

Teaching Strategies for Reading and Writing Workshops

David Hornsby   Jo-Ann Parry   Deborah Sukarna

Colleen Hornsby
Mary McDonald
Bronwen Scarffe
Lesley WingJan

HEINEMANN
Portsmouth, NH

The authors would like to acknowledge the assistance of Gary Chapman, Alison James and Donna Krenn, who trialled procedures in their classrooms and provided valuable comments and ideas. They also thank the staff and students of Ringwood Heights Primary School for allowing them to illustrate topics with photographs of classes at work.

HEINEMANN
A division of Reed Publishing (USA), Inc.
361 Hanover St.
Portsmouth, NH 03801
Offices and agents throughout the world.

First published in 1992 by Phoenix Education, Australia.

ISBN 0 435 08790 8

Library of Congress Cataloging-in-Publication Data

Hornsby, David.
  Teach on/David Hornsby, Deborah Sukarna, Jo-Ann Parry.
    p. cm.
  ISBN 0-435-08790-8
  1. Language experience approach in education. 2. Teaching.
  I. Sukarna, Deborah. II. Parry,, Jo-Ann. III. title.
  LB 1576,H665 1993
  372.6--dc20

Edited by Bettina Stevenson
Designed by Sharon Carr, Graphic Divine
Cover photograph by Northside Productions, Melbourne
Typeset by Bookset Pty Ltd
Printed in Australia by Australian Print Group, Maryborough

CONTENTS

PREFACE

This is a practical book outlining several teaching strategies and procedures that have been successful in classrooms where whole-language philosophy guides the teacher's program.

Every procedure detailed can be used with a group of children; some may also be appropriate for whole-class instruction. Some will look familiar: they are not new, but have been adapted from well-tried procedures that have been a part of many successful classroom programs; others are more recent in development. All are being used successfully, and the authors provide samples of both teachers' and children's 'work-in-progress'.

The book is an attempt to document current practices in a way that will allow teachers who are 'novices' to pick up and run with the procedures, but will also enable those who are 'voyagers' to fine-tune and extend their practice. In addition, as teachers need to match procedures with purposes and with learners' needs, all can use it to help specific children with particular needs.

Teachers determine children's strengths and needs through ongoing evaluation of language use. They may then refer to the section in each chapter that indicates the children for whom each procedure is applicable; this will help them to plan strategy lessons and to teach effectively. At the same time, their strategy lessons *provide* evaluation contexts, so that evaluation is a continuous process rather than an isolated event. When evaluation and teaching occur together, valuable data can be gathered and used for building children's language profiles (which require assessment contexts to be noted).

Recent understandings about language learning have occasionally been mis-interpreted and unsubstantiated claims have been made about skills teaching. Some teachers began to feel 'guilty' about teaching skills they considered to be important. In fact, the teaching of skills *is* appropriate in the whole-language classroom, and this book helps to show how they can be taught in context.

CHAPTER 1

WHOLE-LANGUAGE STRATEGY LESSONS

DAVID HORNSBY AND JO-ANN PARRY

Whole language and teacher-directed instruction

Some of those who have supported a 'whole-language' approach without a broad understanding of the philosophy have mistakenly believed that teacher-directed instruction is no longer appropriate. And some critics of this approach believe that teachers no longer teach! We know teachers who embrace whole-language philosophy but say that they feel unsure about how teaching groups should be handled. Indeed, many feel 'guilty' when teaching skills they consider to be important. Yet Calkins (1986, p. 165) reminds us that we must not be afraid to teach. 'Out of fear of "taking ownership", teachers desperately avoid teaching.'

We are convinced from our own practice and from observation of effective teachers that the best teaching of skills takes place in the whole-language classroom where the teacher truly understands the purpose of the procedure and the needs of the learners.

Reading and writing strategies

Strategies are *modes of operation,* or what readers and writers *do* when they read or write. What they do is based on their *understandings* of the reading and writing processes, their *attitudes* to reading and writing and their *command* of reading and writing skills.

Reading strategies operate the moment a reader's eyes hit the page. The reader may make certain predictions about what the text is going to say, will sample the print, make further predictions about what is to come and then confirm, modify or reject those predictions, as appropriate. If a prediction is rejected, the reader may reread some text or further sample the print so that self-correction is possible. As meaning develops, new information is integrated with old information; parts of the text may be reread for clarification, to allow consideration of different perspectives or to allow more time for fine-tuning and reflecting.

Reading strategies may be operating even before a book is opened. For example, a reader's strategies will vary according to how or why the book was chosen in the first place. If it was selected for a specific purpose (such as the need to find out more about a particular topic), then certain predictions will have been made even before opening it. These predictions may be based on what the reader expects from different forms of text. If the text is expected to be a report or a letter or a procedure, then predictions about its organisation will be made in addition to predictions about its content. If a novel is selected at random, with no particular purpose other than reading for enjoyment, few specific predictions about content may be made, but the reader will almost certainly predict that it will be a narrative or a recount.

A writer may make certain predictions about what text is going to say and write a first draft to explore the ideas or to express something. Once the first draft is written, it may be reworked and revised as earlier predictions or further intentions are expressed. The writer reads and rereads the developing text. Intended meanings are confirmed. If meaning is not as intended, text is rejected or modified and the writer may self-correct and rewrite. The writer continues to reread for clarification, to allow consideration of different perspectives or to allow more time for fine-tuning and reflecting. Intended meanings have been expressed, but the writer may also discover and express new meanings as the writing proceeds. The 'meaning-making' process is driven by a desire to make sense.

Reading and writing strategies also include the *behaviours* that readers and writers employ. For example, readers may behave in different ways when they fail to understand texts or when they come to words they do not know. Writers may behave in different ways when they are unsure of what they are trying to say or when they cannot spell words they want to use.

Reading/writing strategies may be more or less effective. Learners need to become more *aware* of them (that is, more aware of what they *do* when they read and write) so that they can discover the most effective and most efficient modes of operation.

The procedures described in this book help learners to develop this awareness and to make decisions about the most effective and efficient reading/writing strategies.

Common features of all procedures

Language that supports learners' needs

When a teacher is guided by a whole-language philosophy, the language used in the classroom must support the reader or writer in employing all strategies effectively and efficiently. In other words, it must be natural language (both oral and written), containing all the semantic, syntactic and graphophonemic cues that can be used by readers and writers.

It is the children who shape the language being used or generated in the classroom, so teachers must plan with their learners' needs in mind. For this reason, in outlining the procedures for the selected strategy lessons we have identified the children who may benefit from each one. Sometimes a need arises because English is a second language for the child or the child has a non-English-speaking background. All the procedures are appropriate for children with these needs; in fact, they have often been shown to accelerate language development for such children.

Although strategy lessons must use natural language, they must also build upon the existing strengths of the readers and writers. The strengths are used to help learners develop new strategies or to help them gain more control over their use of those already being employed.

When preparing strategy lessons, teachers plan to have children use their reading and writing strengths in order to help them develop aspects of written language for which they need support.

Language awareness

Strategy lessons should also help learners to become more aware of the reading and writing processes and to *articulate* their understandings about reading and writing strategies and about how our language works. A lesson may sometimes be used to *focus* upon one strategy but the procedures usually require the use of several, since several usually operate interdependently. Children will actually talk about reading and writing and become more capable of describing what they *do* when they read and write. They learn to do this because the teacher talks with them at the 'teachable moment' — the moment when they need the information and can make immediate use of it.

The teachable moment is not always easy to predict. However, such moments are more likely to occur in classrooms where teachers and learners are equal and active participants in the learning process, and during the procedures themselves there will be certain times when teachable moments are more likely to appear. By using the two-column format in the 'Procedure' section of each chapter, we have tried to show where they are more likely to occur. Sample questions are often provided in the 'Teacher action' column at these times.

A cycle: Language use ◆ Evaluation ◆ Strategy lesson

Evaluation is a continuous process rather than an isolated event.

It is essential for the teacher to have a curriculum framework that recognises the interrelationships between language use, evaluation and instruction. Teachers must evaluate specific learners' use of language and determine their strengths as well as their needs. This is done by evaluating language as it is being used by learners who are reading and writing for authentic purposes.

Evaluation is a continuous process rather than an isolated event.

As language use is evaluated, teachers receive information that enables them to plan specific lessons for children who need to experience and practise particular reading/writing strategies. When they have identified the children's needs, they may refer to the section 'Children for whom the procedure is applicable'.

Teachers also need to be aware of the need to evaluate their programs so that a balance is achieved. With each procedure, a list of 'features' is given that may help them to consider the range of language experiences they are providing.

Strategy lessons with individuals, groups or whole class

Through continuous evaluation, teachers are able to plan appropriate instruction for individuals or groups. Sometimes it will also be appropriate not to focus upon the strategies or skills, but to model the *procedure* for the whole class; once children know the procedure and its routines, the teacher will probably have less need to work with the whole class, but instead can work with small groups to focus upon the skills, strategies and behaviours.

The teacher may *require* certain children to attend a strategy lesson; others may be *invited* to attend after a brief explanation of purposes has been given. Obviously, the teacher needs to be clear about what he or she is trying to achieve and must communicate this effectively to the children. When this is done, and when invitation is a common phenomenon in the classroom, children will often choose to attend.

Teachers no longer just 'do' a reading or writing activity for the sake of activity. Purposes are clear and are communicated to the learners, who then have clearer expectations and clearer ideas about what they need to do.

When classrooms operate in this way and when teachers and children are equal and active participants, the children are able to become self-directed learners who may then monitor their own development.

Organisation of chapters

A different procedure — and variations of it — is considered in each chapter. In general, we have adopted the following structure.

Features of the procedure
* background information
* the strategies that are practised/learned

Children for whom the procedure is applicable
* related to purpose of procedure
* related to children's needs

Size of group
* often small groups (when focusing upon strategies)
* sometimes individuals (when focusing upon strategies)
* sometimes the whole class (when teaching the procedure)

Materials and preparation
* general statement
* special needs

Procedure
* generally set out in columns for 'teacher action' and 'pupil action'

Other applications

Classroom example
* where possible, a practical example of the procedure

References

Reference

Calkins, Lucy M. 1986, *The Art of Teaching Writing*, Heinemann, Portsmouth, NH.

CHAPTER 2

CLOZE

DAVID HORNSBY

Features of cloze

Cloze refers to the 'reading closure' practice required when readers must fill blanks left in text, using whatever knowledge and experience they have. The strategies needed appear to be the same as those used during reading: thus, cloze exercises can be used to help children develop and refine reading strategies.

Words or letters can be deleted from text in ways that require readers to employ specific reading strategies or to focus upon specific cues in the text. A strength of cloze exercises is that they can be constructed in various ways so that readers must find different textual cues or use different reading strategies: in one way to give practice in using cues and strategies with which children are already familiar; in another way to require them to use cues or develop strategies they overlook.

As with all teaching/learning procedures, cloze activities are best designed by *teachers* since they will know their children. If they know that certain children need practice in sampling graphophonic cues more carefully, they will design a cloze activity different from the one for children who rely too much upon graphophonic cues. Cloze activities can be tailored to suit children's needs; once teachers know what these are, they will design activities appropriately.

Since readers must contribute personally to cloze activities, they learn that what they have to offer is essential to the meaning being constructed as they read. Reading is not a passive activity; it requires active participation and critical thought.

Cloze procedures are also valuable in evaluating reading ability and the appropriateness of text (see 'Other applications').

Children for whom cloze is applicable

Children who don't realise that an active search for meaning has priority in reading.

Children who don't realise that an essential reading strategy is 'educated guessing' or prediction.

Children who need confidence to use what they know already and to apply it to meaning-making as they read.

Children who are not aware of the reading strategies they employ.

Children who rely too much upon one cue in text.

Children who read word by word, but with little or no understanding.

Careless readers who make too many omissions, reversals or insertions.

Non-thinking readers who need to be encouraged to discuss their reading and to become more critical.

Good readers who need to be encouraged to discuss word choice.

Children who don't realise that both non-visual information (including 'what you have in your head') and visual information (including both text and illustration) are essential in reading.

Size of group

Cloze activities are best conducted in small groups. They also can be done with individuals who need specific, one-to-one assistance.

Materials and preparation

It is essential that all materials used for cloze activities are natural, 'authentic' texts so that they support readers in their attempts to construct meaning. Authentic text contains cues and redundancies that help readers to build meaning and to identify unknown words (see Goodman 1968, 1973; Goodman et al. 1987; Smith 1971, 1978, 1982). In fact, if authors suspect that particular concepts and the labels for those concepts (words) are unfamiliar, they endeavour to provide even more cues to assist the reader's meaning-making.

The materials should be relevant to the children and at appropriate levels of difficulty. They may be either commercial texts (stories, short selections, poems, reference works) or classroom materials (language-experience texts, wall stories, selections from children's own writing).

Length of passage

> Cloze activities should be based on passages of text rather than on single sentences.

Context cues (semantic and syntactic) lie in the text surrounding a deletion (including sentences both before and after the one containing the deletion); therefore, cloze activities should be based on *passages* rather than on single sentences. The length of the passage will depend upon the children's stage of reading development.

The first sentence is always left intact, and for emergent and early readers it is usually appropriate to leave intact not only the first one but a few of those following, so that sufficient context has been built up before deletions occur. Then, if only one word is deleted in every fifteen to twenty, several sentences more will be required to make the activity worthwhile; consequently, we believe that cloze activities require passages of at least eight to ten sentences, but also that a maximum be set for the amount of text to be used. Most sources suggest a maximum of 250 to 300 words, although longer texts with a lower deletion rate have been used effectively. Short stories (including both contemporary and traditional tales) and extracts from longer texts are appropriate, and some selections from reading schemes (only those which contain literary merit!) are also useful.

Preparation

The way in which cloze passages are prepared is determined by the purpose of the activity.

* Delete *content* words (such as nouns, verbs, adjectives, adverbs) to encourage the use of **semantic** cues. (Proper nouns are usually left in.)
* Delete *function* words or structure words (such as conjunctions, pronouns, noun determiners, prepositions, verb auxiliaries) to encourage the use of **syntactic** cues. Inflectional and derivational endings used to indicate grammatical changes can also be deleted.
* Delete *letters* or *letter clusters* to encourage the use of **graphophonic** cues.
* Delete words (and sometimes letters or letter clusters) on a regular basis to encourage the use of all language cues. Classification and purpose of words to be deleted and guidelines for the frequency of deletion are given below.

Content words frequently carry meaning even when they are used alone (for instance, dog, walk, happy, quickly). It is often possible to add to the base word an inflectional ending (added to a content word as it joins with other words in a sentence) or a derivational ending (which 'derives' one part of speech from another).

Some common inflectional endings are -s, -es, -ing and -ed:

* for plurals (as in dogs);
* for possessives (as in dog's);
* for past tense (as in walked).

There are many derivational endings. Common endings for **nouns** include -ance, -ant, -ee, -er, -ism, -ist, -ity, -ment, -ness, -sion, -ure. Some common endings for **adjectives** are -able, -al, -er, -est, -ful, -ic, -ish, -ive, -less, -ous. Common **verb** endings are -ate, -en, -ise and -ize, and **adverb** endings include -ly, -wards, -wide and -wise.

Words can often be classified according to their form and function within a sentence; such classes can frequently be given the traditional labels that refer to parts of speech (noun, verb, preposition and so on). It is not possible to classify *single words*, as their classification is partly determined by their function in a sentence. In fact, some words can be classified in several ways, as shown in an example from Emmitt & Pollock (p. 86).

* One *round* is enough (noun).
* You *round* the bends too quickly (verb).
* A *round* tower (adjective).
* He came *round* (adverb).
* He wandered *round* the table (preposition).

Function words have meaning only when they are used with content words. Function words either stand for content words or 'hold them together' in sentences. They are important for providing the syntactic structure of a sentence.

Noun determiners signal that a noun is to follow. Some of the most common are:

* articles — definite (the) and indefinite (a, an);
* cardinal numbers — one, two, three and so on;
* demonstratives — this, these, that or those;
* possessives — my, our, your, his, her, its or their;
* miscellaneous — all, any, both, each, either, few, many, most, no, other, some.

Matching children and texts

It is important for teachers to use their knowledge of the children and to match texts to their needs and capabilities. While some trial and error may be required, there are nevertheless valuable sets of information upon which teachers can draw to make their decisions.

As well as choosing the classes of words or groups of letters to be deleted, the rate of deletion needs to be considered. There is no set rate; it is determined by the stage of development of the children and the 'conceptual load' of the text. A very rough rule of thumb is as follows:

Stage of development	Maximum rate of deletion
Emergent	1 in 15–20 words
Early	1 in 12–15 words
Developing	1 in 8–10 words
Fluent	1 in 5–8 words

Remember that these rates provide only a rough guideline when the children are reading materials that would be considered as 'independent' for them; the rate would be even lower when they are reading 'instructional' materials.

If the text is about a familiar subject, more words could be deleted than if it is unfamiliar.

It is important to remember that the activity is to help the reader with reading strategies. The aim is to use those strategies to complete the deletions successfully and to be able to articulate what was done and why. The aim is *not* to make the procedure a test or to make it as difficult as possible.

Generally, the deleted words are replaced by lines of equal length. Teachers could use lines that exactly represent the length of deletions if they want each response to be the original word, but most cloze applications accept synonyms. Only in testing situations (see p. 14) are exact replacements required.

Procedure

There are several useful cloze procedures, all of which are valuable for different reasons. They could be categorised as follows:

1 oral

2 written

3 modified (see 'Other applications')

1   Oral cloze

Teacher action

Teacher introduces text (short story or selection from a book). Teacher reads title of book or selection and asks children what they think is going to happen.

Teacher reads to the first deletion and asks children to suggest a word that might come next.

When children have predicted a word, teacher asks: 'Why do you choose that word?'. Teacher either confirms prediction or asks why it could not be right. Teacher encourages discussion of alternatives.

Teacher reads to the next deletion, pauses, looks expectantly at the children.

Pupil action

Children make predictions about the text. This also helps to set purposes for the shared reading. Children discuss their different predictions.

Children consider their predictions and use the extra context they have picked up from the teacher's oral reading to suggest a word.

Children have to justify their choice of word, using not only information from the text and any illustrations, but also their own knowledge. They predict and consider alternatives.

Children continue as above.

The cycle of
Predicting → Justifiying → Comparing → Discussing
is continued until the passage is completed.

Oral cloze of this kind needs to be planned in advance. During the preparation teachers should decide upon the words to be deleted, but should subsequently make changes according to how well the children are coping with the task. The frequency of the deletions must be low enough to ensure that the 'flow' of the story is not lost.

It is appropriate to use an overhead projector so that children see the text as the teachers read it. Words to be deleted are simply covered with 'Post-it' notes. After the children have made predictions and justified them, the notes can be peeled off to reveal the word the author used. Sometimes children can give good reasons for preferring *their* words to the author's.

2 Written cloze

With the first sentence or two left intact so that readers can cue into the context of the passage, words will be deleted according to your purpose. Generally, proper nouns are not deleted.

(a) Children are encouraged to read through the entire passage quickly.
(b) Children then go back to the beginning and start filling in the blanks. They don't have to do this in order; they may backtrack.
(c) Children are encouraged to reread the whole passage, with two main questions in mind: 'Does this sound right?' and 'Does it make sense to me?'. *Note*: All responses that make sense are accepted. Wrong spellings do not count against the child.
(d) Children compare their responses with the original words in the passage. Discussion that focuses on whether or not the author's intended meaning is affected by acceptance of the children's responses is most worthwhile.
(e) The Predicting → Justifying → Comparing → Discussing cycle continues.

Other applications

Co-operative group cloze

This is an adaptation of oral cloze.
1 All read the passage together (orally) until the first deletion is reached.
2 Members of the group are encouraged to recommend words.
3 Members challenge each other with questions such as 'Why do you think it could be that word?' until the group reaches a consensus about the 'best' replacement word.
4 All children write this word on their own copies of the text.
5 Members of the group read to the next deletion and the cycle starts again.

Last-word cloze

With emergent and early readers, return to a favourite 'Big Book'. Before the session, delete the last word of each sentence — where it is highly predictable — by covering it with card (using Blu-tak) or with 'Post-it' notes.

Concept clarification

With older readers, delete words that require children to draw upon their knowledge of a particular topic or subject. This can be useful for revising curriculum content. When completed as a co-operative group activity, members of the group may share their knowledge, perceptions and insights.

Poetry cloze

Dylan Thomas wrote: 'The best craftsmanship always leaves holes and gaps in the works of the poem so that something that is NOT in the poem can creep, crawl, flash or thunder in'. Leave the first verse intact; delete words from those following. Children, in pairs or small groups, should now be given plenty of time to 'listen' to their replacement words. They may let them creep, crawl, flash or thunder in! In a poem they must not only fit the intended meaning, but also the form and 'flow' of the poetry. Deletions can require them to focus upon particular images, upon rhyme and rhythm or upon patterns of word use.

Cloze as an evaluation instrument

Obviously, when teachers tune in to children's discussion regarding the choice of replacement words and the justifications made, they receive extremely valuable feedback regarding learning. They are able to evaluate not only content, but how children process that content. Information about how the children process language allows teachers to design the specific types of cloze activity that individuals need and also to identify students for whom further cloze work will be appropriate (see page 8).

Cloze as a method of determining the readability level of text

Cloze can be a rough indicator of whether a passage is at an independent level, an instructional level or a frustration level for children in the middle and upper grades. The normal procedure for estimating these levels is as follows.

1 Select a passage of about 300 words. Leave the first sentence intact, then delete every fifth word until there are fifty deletions. Do not delete proper nouns or the first word of any sentence.

2 Prepare the passage with blanks of uniform length in place of the deleted words.

3 Administer as a test. The children do not have to fill the gaps in order and spelling mistakes are not penalised.

4 Mark the passage. Accept only the exact words deleted. Multiply the score out of 50 by 2 to gain a percentage mark.

For younger children, it may be advisable to delete only every seventh word and so have fewer than fifty deletions, but more difficult mathematics will be required to work out the percentage!

Score (%):   0 ◄────▼────► 40 ◄────▼────► 60 ◄────▼────► 100
Level: Frustration   Instruction   Independence

If a score between 40 per cent and 60 per cent is obtained, the child should be able to manage the text with the teacher's assistance in a guided reading situation. If a score of 60 to 65 per cent or more is obtained, the child should be able to read the text independently. Research indicates that this typical methodology gives adequate results (Bormuth 1963); Elley, in a paper written in the 1980s, believes that 'there is little doubt now that the cloze procedure is a sensitive measure of reading difficulty' when the orthodox procedure is followed. Yet while information from a cloze test may be valuable, we caution the reader that the teacher is still the best judge of a child's reading ability and the best person to match reader and text appropriately.

Classroom example

These sample cloze passages are taken from *The Hungry Chickens*, a traditional rhyme.

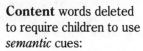

Content words deleted to require children to use *semantic* cues:

Page 2
The first chicken said with a sad, little squirm, I can only find this skinny, little worm.

Page 4
The second _____ said with a funny, little shrug,

Page 5
I can only find this nasty, little _____ .

Page 6
The third chicken said with a sharp, _____ squeal,

Page 7
I can only find this old lemon _____ .

Page 8
The fourth chicken _____ with a tired, little moan,

Page 9
I can only find this hard, little stone.

Page 10
The _____ chicken said with a little cry of grief,

Page 11
I can only _____ this little, green _____ .

Page 12
Now, look here! said Mother Hen from the green garden patch.

Page 14
If you _____ any breakfast, you come here and . . .

Page 16
scratch!

Function words deleted to require children to use *syntactic* cues:

Page 2
The first chicken said with a sad, little squirm, I can only find this skinny, little worm.

Page 4
The second chicken said with _____ funny, little shrug,

Page 5
I can only find this nasty, little slug.

Page 6
The third chicken said _____ a sharp, little squeal,

Page 7
I can only find _____ old lemon peel.

Page 8
_____ fourth chicken said with a tired, little moan,

Page 9
_____ can only find this hard, little stone.

Page 10
The fifth chicken said with a little cry _____ grief,

Page 11
I can only find this little, green leaf.

Page 12
Now, look here! said Mother Hen _____ the green garden patch.

Page 14
If you want any breakfast, _____ come here and . . .

Page 16
scratch!

Letters or **letter clusters** deleted to require children to use *graphophonic* knowledge:

Page 2
The first chicken said with a sad, little squirm, I can only find this skinny, little worm.

Page 4
The second _____icken said with a funny, little shrug,

Page 5
I can only find this nasty, little sl_____ .

Page 6
The third chicken said with a sharp, _____ittle squeal,

Page 7
I can only find this old lemon pee____ .

This example might be continued to emphasise initial and final letters and letter clusters. However, the teacher may also wish to emphasise medial letters or clusters, or may focus upon single consonants or consonant clusters (such as sk, sl, sm, sn, sp). Larger clusters containing consonants and vowels (ead, eaf, eak, eam and so on) help children to develop visual memory for these common units and therefore also assist in the development of spelling.

Decisions about deletions must depend upon the needs of the children in the group.

References

Bormuth, John R. 1963, 'Cloze as a measure of readability', *Proceedings*, International Reading Association, 8: 131–4.

Cambourne, Brian 1977, 'Some psycholinguistic dimensions of the silent reading process', Ridsdale, A., Ryan, D. & Horan, J. (eds), *Literacy for Life*, Proceedings of the Third Australian Reading Conference, Melbourne.

Elley, Warwick (n.d., 1980s), 'A close look at the cloze test', *Set: Research Information for Teachers*, special issue, New Zealand Council of Educational Research.

Emmitt, M. & Pollock, J. 1991, *Language and Learning*, Oxford University Press, Melbourne.

Goodman, Kenneth (ed.) 1968, 1973, *The Psycholinguistic Nature of the Reading Process*, Wayne State University Press, Detroit.

Goodman, Kenneth, Brooks Smith, E., Meredith, Robert & Goodman, Yetta 1987, *Language and Thinking in School: A Whole-language Curriculum*, Richard C. Owen, New York.

The Hungry Chickens, a traditional rhyme illustrated by Kathryn Pond, Literacy 2000, Rigby Education, Crystal Lake, Illinois.

Kemp, Max 1980, *Reading/Language Processes: Assessment and Teaching*, Australian Reading Association, Adelaide.

Smith, Frank 1971, 1978, 1982, *Understanding Reading*, Erlbaum, Hillsdale, NJ.

Weaver, Constance 1979, *Reading Process and Practice: From Sociopsycholinguistics to Whole Language*, Heinemann, Portsmouth.

CHAPTER 3

DATA CHARTS

DEBORAH SUKARNA AND DAVID HORNSBY

Features of data charts

A data chart gives children visual means of organising different information about the same topic from different non-fiction references.

Children are required to learn and use summarising skills.

Children are required to synthesise the information from the data chart and write it in their own words.

The procedure builds upon what children already know or believe about a particular topic.

Children learn the importance of research.

Children come to understand that it is important to consider various reference books, other texts and resources (videos, guest speakers, charts) when researching a topic.

The procedure helps to define purposes for reading, which include reading for information from text, reading for information from non-text graphics (such as charts, maps, photographs, graphs or diagrams), reading for confirmation and reading to compare and contrast.

Children learn about various forms of non-fiction text organisation.

Children need to use various parts of a publication, such as table of contents, index, glossary, footnotes.

Children are required to 'scan' for specific information and then to decide what is relevant — to distinguish between the key information and trivial points. Key information is read closely.

A data chart is an *outline* of information and provides an excellent overview if a follow-up report is to be written. Data charts are useful preparation if the teacher wishes to construct a report jointly with the group. The charts would be a step towards requiring individual children to write their own reports on the topic.

Data charts can be used to teach children how to compile a bibliography.

Children for whom data charts are applicable

Children who have reached the stage of using non-fiction texts for research. As texts are both oral and written, this will include reading books, listening to audiotapes or visiting speakers, viewing videotapes and so on.

Children who have difficulty synthesising information from various sources.

Children who fail to realise how important this synthesis is for comprehension based on all points of view available through the various texts.

Children who do not know how to use the various features of non-fiction texts to advantage.

Children who lack confidence in their use of non-fiction texts.

Children who fail to understand the need for careful research before writing.

Children who fail to use an adequate number and variety of resources for their research.

Children who need to organise information before writing a report.

Children who do not choose to read non-fiction books.

Children who need help with summarising.

Children who transcribe chunks of information from reference texts when researching or investigating an area of study.

Materials and preparation

The data chart usually draws upon the content of a unit of work in progress. If it is an integrated unit, the content comes from social education, science, health and environmental education. We express our understanding of the content through language, drama, music, mathematics, art/craft and so on; however, it is the use of *language* to process information with which we are concerned here. (An extremely valuable reference is *The Big Picture: Integrated Curriculum*, edited by Keith Pigdon and Marilyn Woolley.

The materials will be the references related to the unit of work, which may include books, videotapes, filmstrips, charts and any other printed or visual source. Notes from guest speakers, excursions and other shared experiences may also constitute relevant text for this procedure.

Equipment required includes:

* large sheets of blank paper;
* a large, whole-class data chart (the teacher creates this chart as the procedure progresses);
* paper for children to prepare their own data charts, or prepared forms ready for use.

Procedure

The procedure outlined may be taught as a valuable way of synthesising information from a variety of sources. It is necessary to do this as a *series* of 'mini-lessons' during language workshops. The example used is from a Year 5 unit on early Australian transport.

The outline given here is for whole-class sessions. Once students know the procedure they ought to use it independently — or working with partners — to help them process their information. Through observation, teachers will be able to determine which of them may need extra help either with the procedure itself or with the skills (such as summarising) required to complete it. This help would be provided through teaching groups during the language workshop.

First session

Teacher action

Teacher takes a topic from a new or current unit of work and asks, 'What do we know about this topic?', 'What do we think we know?'.

Teacher lists on large sheets of paper what children believe about the topic. When necessary, teacher asks questions to elicit further information.

Teacher now asks, 'What do we want to find out?' and lists children's questions.

Teacher asks children to group similar items together (from both 'What we know' and 'What we want to find out'). Teacher assists them with labels if necessary.

Pupil action

Children share what they know about the topic (e.g. riverboats were an important form of transport on the Murray River). They listen to one another for information that will 'trigger' other things they know about the topic.

Children are encouraged to challenge beliefs put forward by others. A belief on which there is no consensus is marked for later consideration.

Children usually indicate what they want to find out by posing questions (e.g. *when* were riverboats first used on the Murray River?).

Children identify items that belong together. Individual items are cut from the sheets of paper and grouped. Groupings may change as children discuss the information. Each group is given a label, which becomes a heading on the data chart.

Second session

Note: when first teaching this procedure, the first two steps are *demonstrated by the teacher*. Later, children will complete these steps themselves.

Teacher action

Teacher prepares a large, blank data chart (on paper or chalkboard) for demonstration purposes. Small, individual copies are duplicated for the children. (See 'Preparation'.)

Teacher explains that the data chart is going to be used to organise all the information gathered.

'Group labels' now become headings across the top of the data chart and the teacher writes them in. It may be necessary to focus the research and limit the number of headings.

Teacher points out that the top row of the data chart is for 'what we believe or know', but that information is to be checked against information from other references.

Pupil action

Children write the headings on their own copies of the data chart. They may have to make a decision about which 'groups of information' they will research.

Children give teacher statements of 'what we believe or know' and teacher writes them on large, whole-class chart. Children transcribe this information on to their own sheets. Later, they will do this independently.

Third session

Teacher action

Teacher explains that the left-hand column is used to list references that will be used to collect information on the subject. Teacher asks, 'Why is it important to use several references when researching a subject?'.

Teacher chooses a reference, reads a relevant extract aloud, demonstrates how to compose a summary statement of it and writes the summary on the data chart. (Statements are usually phrases rather than complete sentences.)

Teacher asks children to search another reference for additional information for the data charts. When the procedure is new to them, the references may be provided and may be limited in number. When it is familiar, they will be expected to select their own references and provide the necessary details in the left-hand column of the data chart.

Pupil action

Children discuss reasons for using several references, including videos, visiting speakers and notes from excursions, as well as text books.

After the teacher has demonstrated summarising skills, the children summarise *with* the teacher. Common abbreviations should be used and specific abbreviations for the current topic can be determined.

Children choose a reference from those available. They record its title and other information in the left-hand column. They read the reference, keeping the headings in mind, and jot down key words, phrases or summary statements in the appropriate boxes on the chart. This could be done in pairs.

Teacher action

Teacher may fill in the large demonstration chart if it is to be used as an overall summary of the class findings.

Pupil action

Children record information from other references only if it has not been recorded previously. If no additional information is found from a particular reference, the box can be crossed.

DATA CHART   Topic : Riverboats

Headings	DESCRIPTION	MOVEMENT	PURPOSES
What I/we already know	Steering poles Wet redgum swells		
Reference 1 **Coaches, Riverboats & Railways** 994 HOW	Redgum hulls — withstand impact Side + stern-wheelers Shallow draught Tow barges	Easy to handle around bends Speedy — faster than bullocks Smoother journey than bullocks	Trade — wool, sheep Goods — perfume to butter churns Reduced isolation Supplies for gold diggings Snaggers
Reference 2 **The Book** of Australia pp 218-9	Some outrigger barges Passenger boats — electric light + hot showers Steam engine		Passengers Mission boats — chapels Hawkers Clothing makers Fishing Timber
Reference 3 **Riverboats** 386 DUG	Paddles attached to wheels Paddle wheels not deep in water Wood fuel	Force of paddles moved boats Often stopped for wood Bargemaster steered barge	Provisions for farmers

Further sessions

Once the data chart is completed it is an excellent overview of information about the topic being researched, for which there will be notes under the specific headings that were determined during the first session. The information from the references should be used to confirm, question or reject what was written under 'What we believe (or know)'.

Name: J5G		Date begun: 12·2·92
HISTORY	DECLINE	RIVER SYSTEM
1853: Mary Ann — 1st P.S. 1865: 27 Riverboats 1880: 20,000 tonnes of wool through Echuca Changed lives of inland settlers	Riverboats peaked during 1870s River trade gone – 1900s Became less profitable Railways took over — cheaper + quicker	Murray River system covers ⅓ of Australia Fine pasture land Floods + droughts Planned for 'Nile of Australia' Many wharves + ports
Great days of river- boats lasted 30 years Boats fly Murray River flag 1853: Famous race 1850: Biggest wool cargo		Rivers — trade highways 6500 km of river
Best type of transport 1850s : farms along Murray 1870s : Echuca major port Crew – captain, mate, deckhands, engineer, cook, fireman	1940s: Last riverboat company closed WWI – Long drought Motor cars + roads	Many bends — hard to navigate

The children are now required to read down a column and consider all the information listed under one heading. This may be done by individuals or pairs. Related information should be synthesised and written in complete sentences until all relevant facts about that particular aspect of the topic are covered. The children then go on with the other aspects of the topic, according to the headings on their data charts.

HISTORY

In 1853 the first paddle steamer was named Mary Ann.

In 1865 there were 27 riverboats on the river.

20,000 tonnes of wool passed through Echuca in 1880.

Riverboats changed the lives of inland settlers.

The great days of riverboats lasted for 30 years.

Each boat flew the Murray River flag.

A famous race was held in 1853.

In 1850 the biggest wool cargo was hauled up the river.

Riverboats were the best type of transport.

In the 1850s there were farms all along the Murray.

Echuca was the major river port in the 1870s.

The crew of a riverboat was a captain, mate, deckhand, engineer, cook and fireman.

Revision will probably be necessary to improve the writing and children may need to return to references to check their information. They may need to revise the order in which it is written, improve word use, attend to sentence structure and so on. Since the *purpose* of the writing is to document, organise and communicate factual information, it will be written as a *report*; children should already be familiar with the way in which text is organised in a report and with its typical language features. During revision, they will check the organisation of their text and their language use (see Derewianka 1990; WingJan 1991.) It will also be necessary to consider the use of illustrations, photographs, maps, charts and other non-text information. The left-hand column of the data chart, which lists the references, can be used to teach how to compile a bibliography.

In 1853 the Mary Ann was the first riverboat on the Murray. It was involved in a famous race. Riverboats soon changed the lives of settlers by opening up the inland, and by the 1850s there were many farms along the Murray.
Riverboats proved to be the best type of transport, and by 1865 twenty-seven riverboats were on the river. The number of riverboats increased, and by the 1870s Echuca was a major Australian port.

NEXT STEP
↓

Revise so that you have a short, polished paragraph.

Other applications

Younger, dependent readers can benefit from a large, whole-class data chart. For example, the teacher may share a non-fiction text with the class and write statements about the chosen topic on large strips which students can place under the appropriate headings on the data chart. Whenever possible, students should be required to illustrate their understandings of the topic and to add their illustrations to the data chart. The teacher will also share another non-fiction text and write statements to add to those previously recorded. At this stage, two references may be sufficient.

Because of the size of both the written statements and the students' illustrations, it may be necessary to break the data chart up into sections for display purposes — for example, you may need to draw up a separate chart for each reference or for each 'subtopic'.

Communicating information

Students can be encouraged to brainstorm ways in which the information in the data chart can be communicated to others. Apart from a written information report, it may be appropriate to consider such things as:
* oral presentation, drama, role play;
* booklet, 'big book', concertina book;
* posters, charts;
* murals, dioramas, collage, constructions, mobiles;
* multimedia kit (videotape, audiotape, pictures, slides and so on).

References

Derewianka, Beverly 1990, *Exploring How Texts Work*, Primary English Teaching Association, Rozelle, NSW.

Pigdon, Keith & Woolley, Marilyn 1993, *The Big Picture: Integrated Curriculum*, Heinemann Educational Books Inc., Portsmouth NH.

WingJan, Lesley 1991, *Write Ways: Modelling Writing Forms*, Oxford University Press, Melbourne.

CHAPTER 4

DIRECTED READING- THINKING ACTIVITIES (DRTA)

JO-ANN PARRY

Features of DRTA

DRTA is a problem-solving approach to reading that may be used with either fiction or non-fiction material.

The purposes for reading are set by the readers.

The teacher has an active role that requires provocative questioning to challenge readers.

The procedure develops reasoning abilities and self-monitoring behaviours so that they become reading *habits*.

The procedure is competency-based (it requires a group of children of similar reading ability).

Children for whom DRTA is applicable

Readers who need to be more conscious of the role of prediction in reading.

Non-thinking readers who need to be encouraged to discuss their reading and become more critical.

Children who read in small 'chunks' (that is, who read word by word or sentence by sentence) and who need to think at 'whole text' level.

Readers who lack perseverance with longer text.

Children who need to learn or practise 'skimming and scanning' skills.

Size of group

DRTA is best conducted with six to eight children, but the group may be as large as ten or twelve with older and more experienced readers if time allows all to be involved.

Materials and preparation

One piece of text is read by all in the group; multiple copies are therefore needed. Since all are to read the same text in roughly the same time, material selected needs to be at an independent level for their stage of development.

The reading material must be *unknown*, as features of the procedure are prediction and problem-solving. (If after beginning to read children discover that they know the text, they quietly go to another activity.)

It is essential for teachers to prepare the material before the session. They should read the entire selection, decide upon possible stopping points for prediction, reflection and discussion, and make copies as required. We have found it helpful, when the procedure is new to children, to actually cut the text into the sections and then to repaste and copy, so that each section is on a separate page or two.

Narrative is used most often for this procedure, but non-fiction may also be used. In either case, the material must be of high quality.

Narrative must have a strong plot and children should have experienced the form chosen (fable, fairy story, legend, mystery, tall story and so on). Since most of them have experience of folk tales, lesser known or contemporary tales are often good places to start. (But remember that the material should be unfamiliar.) The narrative should also have identifiable episodes, so that reading can stop at the end of one episode to allow reflection and discussion before making predictions about the next.

Non-fiction must focus on subject matter that is intrinsically interesting to the children; in other words, it may often be linked to current interests or work in progress. The genre should be familiar and the text a good example of that genre in terms of structure.

Length of text

Short texts are ideal for this procedure. However, for narrative the text does need to have a strong plot and several episodes, and for non-fiction to have information separable into sections.

The number of times reading is stopped will be determined according to the experience of the readers, their reading development and the complexity of the material. There are usually between three and five breaks, but for younger children or for those just learning the procedure it may be sufficient to break just twice.

While it is important to plan the breaks before the session, teachers may vary them to respond to readers' needs. The need to be flexible is more important when using the procedure orally.

Choice of text

Since short texts are ideal, good sources for material include:
* school magazines;
* selections from graded reading programs (only those that have literary merit!);
* traditional tales;
* general miscellanies or anthologies.

Procedure

The procedure is based on the following cycle, which is repeated with each section of the text.

Teacher action	Pupil action
Activate thought. (What do you think?)	Predict. (Set purposes.)
Agitate thought. (Why do you think so?)	Read. (Process ideas.)
Require evidence. (Prove it!)	Prove. (Test answers.)

Source: Stauffer 1975.

Teacher action

Teacher distributes text. Reads title or asks children to read it.

Teacher *activates* by asking what the story might be about (to encourage prediction at 'whole story' level).

Teachers *agitates* thought by asking for reasons for predictions, receiving all responses non-judgmentally. Teacher encourages all children to contribute.

Teacher encourages children to look at any illustrations.

Pupil action

Children predict and thereby set purposes for their reading.

All children volunteer a prediction or an opinion.

Children check their predictions with the additional information from illustrations.

Teacher action	*Pupil action*
Teacher asks children to read to first 'stop' and to reflect upon and restate earlier predictions.	Children read silently. After reading, they review their predictions.
Teacher *requires* individuals to read from the text any part that supports their predictions or any part that causes them to modify or reject their predictions.	Children read orally and comment. (They 'prove' their predictions, or modify and change them.)
Teacher *activates* cycle again by asking for any new predictions based on the new information read. Teacher *agitates* again by asking, 'Why do you think so?'.	Children *predict*, and justify their predictions. Sometimes justification is made by reading orally from earlier text. Shared discussion follows.
Teacher asks children to read to the second 'stop' and to reflect upon and restate earlier predictions. (The second and following sections of text are usually longer than the first.)	Children read silently. After reading, they review their predictions and shared discussion follows again.

> This cycle continues until all sections of text are read.

There are usually four or five stops in total. The final stop should be close to the end, but just before the conclusion or summary. (If reading a narrative, the final stop will be at or just before the climax, so that predictions are made about the resolution.)

Final step

The group, with the teacher, express feelings about the mood of the text, the styles of writing and any major themes. Anything that surprised them will also be discussed here. It may also be appropriate to discuss particular use of words.

Oral or written DRTAs

Although the procedure outlined refers to DRTAs where the written text is read silently by individual group members, it is also possible to have the teacher read the text aloud while group members follow on their own copies of the text or an overhead transparency. Reading the text orally is particularly relevant for emergent and early readers or non-confident readers.

Other applications

Writing predictions

In the procedure as outlined, the children predict and justify their predictions orally. It is also possible to have them write their predictions. Teachers may decide that this is appropriate when groups of older children are all working at the one time.

Click or clunk?

This is a procedure for self-monitoring of reading. Readers are encouraged to stop at the end of each paragraph or section of text and to ask themselves: 'Does this click for me, or does it clunk?'. It 'clicks' if the reader can make sense of the paragraph. It 'clunks' if the meaning is unclear, and the reader then needs to ask, 'Why doesn't this click for me?' and to decide what to do to make the message clearer. This simple but effective procedure is similar to personalised DRTA (see Weaver 1988).

Individual DRTAs

Once children have been involved in small-group DRTAs, it may be appropriate for the teacher to spend time with individuals who have not been able to participate in group activities.

Individual DRTAs allow for shifts in pacing. The teacher may slow the pace when the child requires more reading-thinking time or accelerate it when he or she needs to be challenged. Individual DRTAs also allow for child self-selection of material, 'attentive sharing' between teacher and child, and closer evaluation of the child's reading skills and strategies.

Paired DRTAs

This procedure operates well where there is a strong sense of classroom co-operation and team spirit; children in pairs (including peer tutoring, cross-age tutoring and buddy systems) work together following the cycle described in the procedure.

DRTAs used for evaluation

DRTAs (both group and individual) allow teachers to observe many of the reading skills and strategies in action. They are particularly helpful when teachers wish to monitor the way in which children predict (are they capable of predicting at the 'whole text' level?) and how they use what they comprehend to justify their predictions. Through observation and questioning, teachers may also gain useful information about children's previous reading experiences and so judge what experiences they may need to provide in the future.

Classroom example

The following example was completed with four children (aged eight) at the beginning of the school year. The procedure was unknown to them. The text used was *Anak the Brave*, from the Sunshine series. Through the transcript, it can be seen how the DRTA cycle repeats throughout the procedure.

Anak the Brave

Story by Judy Ling

Illustrations by Chris Rothero

TEACHER:	The title of the story is *Anak the Brave*. What do you think that story may be about?
EDWARD:	A brave boy.
MARCUS:	A boy and his pets and his family.
ABBIE:	He might have some sort of an animal in the jungle.
TEACHER:	You think it has something to do with an animal in the jungle, Abbie? That's an interesting idea. Let's have a look at the front cover. (*Front cover shown.*) Does this give you any more ideas?
KIRSTY:	It *is* about the jungle — and about a boy who probably saves an animal or something.
TEACHER:	Who thinks their predictions could still be possible?
ABBIE:	Mine could still be right.
MARCUS:	It probably isn't about pets; but it could be about a farm boy and his work on the farm.
EDWARD:	I'll stick to my prediction.
TEACHER:	Remember the predictions you have made. I'm going to give you a copy of the book now and I'd like you to read to the end of page 4 and then stop. When you have finished reading, just look up so that we know who has finished. (*Children read text silently.*)
TEACHER:	Having had a chance to read part of the story, what do you think now? Could your prediction still be possible, Abbie?
ABBIE:	Yes.
TEACHER:	From what you have read so far, what makes you think you could be right?

TEACH ON

Anak lived in Borneo on the banks
of a mighty river.
His life was a happy one.
Sometimes he helped his father plant rice.
Sometimes they hunted animals and birds
in the jungle.
But mostly, Anak and his friends played
in the river.
They caught fish, crabs and prawns.
They paddled their canoes.
And in the evening,
they bathed in the river to cool off
after the long hot day.

2

Anak was a small boy, but he had
big dreams.
For as far back as anyone could remember,
Anak's family had been famous warriors.
At night, when the elders
sat on the longhouse verandah
and told stories about Anak's ancestors,
Anak thought to himself, "One day
they will tell such stories about me."
Then he would think,
"First, I must do something brave."

4   5

ABBIE: I'm not sure about it being a jungle, but I know that he could easily
            save an animal. I think that because all the other people in his family
            are warriors.

TEACHER: Are there any words or sentences that you have read so far that
            confirm your prediction?

DIRECTED READING-THINKING ACTIVITIES

EDWARD: I don't know ... ah ... he does say he must do something brave.

KIRSTY: He's in the jungle — it says that on page 1. He hunts for birds.

TEACHER: Marcus, do you think it could still be about a farm boy?

MARCUS: Not really. I think now that he is going around killing animals, because his father and everyone were warriors. He's practising to be a warrior.

TEACHER: Could you read out the part that tells us that?

MARCUS: 'Anak's family had been famous warriors.' [p. 4]

TEACHER: Yes, good. Now Kirsty, did you find the section you were looking for?

KIRSTY: Yes. It says, 'Sometimes they hunted animals and birds in the jungle'. [p. 2]

TEACHER: Does that help you too, Abbie?

ABBIE: Yes. Although it's not really likely that he is going to *save* an animal. It's more likely that he will kill a dangerous animal.

MARCUS: He could be saving nice animals and killing dangerous ones.

TEACHER: Mmm ... it could be. Let's read on a bit and stop at the end of page 8. While you are reading, think about what you have just read and about your predictions, and see if your predictions stay the same.

ABBIE: Well, my prediction could still be the same, because there *is* a dangerous crocodile in the river. Anak could kill it for the people so that they can go back to the river and swim and wash their clothes.

One day, the elders called a meeting of everyone in the longhouse.
"We have heard news of a fierce crocodile in our river," they said.
"Where he came from, no one knows, but he is the worst crocodile in memory. He ate fifteen people last week alone. No one is to go near the river again until we have caught him."

Life became difficult for Anak's people.
They could no longer bathe,
or wash their clothes in the river.
No one knew when the crocodile
would next poke his ugly snout
out of the water.
Anak and his friends were sad.
They could not play in the river
on hot days. And they could no longer
catch sweet river fish, prawns and crabs.
There was nothing much to eat
but rice and vegetables.

"We'll have to do something about this
crocodile," people said. "But what?
He's so cunning, so fierce, so strong!"

TEACHER:	Yes, maybe Anak is going to prove himself.
MARCUS:	He'll be a warrior.
TEACHER:	Could you read the part that tells you that?
ABBIE:	Page 6 tells me that my prediction could be right. (*She then reads page 6.*)
TEACHER:	So, the crocodile *is* causing some problems. Kirsty, what do you think?
KIRSTY:	I think he'll be killing dangerous animals, not saving them.
TEACHER:	Right. So you have changed your prediction a little.
EDWARD:	I think he'll probably kill the crocodile and people will be very thankful and he'll become a warrior.
TEACHER:	What makes you think that Anak will become a warrior? (*Here the teacher is attempting to bring Edward back to the text.*)
EDWARD:	Well, if he kills the crocodile, he'll probably kill something else as well. (*Edward still avoids oral reading to prove his point.*)
TEACHER:	Remember what we have just talked about, and now read to the end of page 16.
TEACHER:	Marcus, you agreed with Edward before. What do you think now?
MARCUS:	Well, Anak is trying to hunt down the crocodile. If he actually kills it, they will say, 'You're a warrior'.
TEACHER:	What makes you think he is prepared to kill the animal?

DIRECTED READING-THINKING ACTIVITIES

Here at last, thought Anak, was a chance
for him to do something brave.
"I'll catch the crocodile!" he said.
"You! You're just a boy!
Not much taller than a blade of grass.
Don't talk nonsense!" the elders laughed.

Anak stayed silent,
but deep in his heart he was angry.
"I'll show them!" he thought.
"I have the blood of warriors
in my veins!"

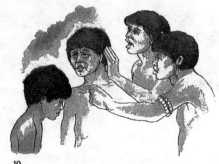

Anak thought for a long time about ways
to catch the crocodile.
Then he remembered something in a place
that his grandfather had shown him
long ago.
Something no-one else knew about.

"You are my eldest grandson,"
the old man had said.
"This secret is my gift to you.
It may be useful to you some day."

10

11

Anak packed a bag with enough food
for a long journey.
He slung it over his back.
He carried a blowpipe and a sharp knife.
He told no one that he was going.
"I must walk up-river for three days
till I reach the rapids," he said
to himself.

12

MARCUS: It says he has a dagger. The book says, 'Anak packed a bag with
           enough food for a long journey. He slung it over his back. He
           carried a blowpipe and a sharp knife'. [p. 12]
KIRSTY: Yes. I think he might use the blowpipe and sharp knife.

TEACH ON

Anak walked from dawn till dusk.
On the way, he met many people
from other longhouses.

"Where are you going?" they asked.
"Such a small boy, all by yourself!"

Anak didn't answer them.
Finally he reached the rapids.
Now came the difficult part.
He turned left along the jungle path.
He wasn't sure of the way.
Nothing looked as it had before
when his grandfather had taken him.
Anak knew he would have to be
very careful,
because there were snakes
and dangerous animals about.
He moved as swiftly and silently
as a mousedeer.

By nightfall, Anak had reached
the limestone cliffs.
He lit a fire to keep wild animals away.
There were strange jungle noises all around.
Anak felt scared and he clutched
his knife and blowpipe close.

ABBIE:	Mmm . . . he said he had something that his grandpa had given him. But we don't know what it is yet. It could be something that could kill a crocodile.
TEACHER:	Could you read that section for us? (*Abbie reads page 11.*)
TEACHER:	So you don't think he will use the knife and blowpipe?
MARCUS:	It could be in that basket. He probably brought the basket for the grandfather's secret weapon.
EDWARD:	(*having referred to the illustration*) Well, it could be tucked down his pants, and the basket is for delicious food.
TEACHER:	How could we find out?
ABBIE:	We need to read more.
TEACHER:	Let's read to the end of page 23.

DIRECTED READING-THINKING ACTIVITIES

When the sun came up, Anak searched
for the hornets' nest that his grandfather
had shown him.
Anak found it high on the cliff face.
Near the hornets' nest, Anak found
his grandfather's secret grove of plants.

"These are the most poisonous plants
in the whole jungle," Grandfather had said.
"One bite is enough to kill
an elephant."

17

Anak plucked some of the plants
and put them in his bag.
Back he went through the jungle
to the rapids, then down-river to his home.
He was hot and tired.

His parents were very angry.
"We looked everywhere for you,"
they said. "We thought you were dead."

"I'm sorry," Anak replied. "But I had
important things to do."

18

19

The next morning Anak got up
before dawn.
He killed a chicken and stuffed
its stomach with the poisonous plants.
Then he tied it to a strong vine.
Standing on the river bank, Anak waited.

Before long, the crocodile spied Anak.
He lunged at the chicken at the end
of Anak's vine. Quick as lightning,
Anak jerked the chicken out of the
crocodile's reach. The crocodile
furiously splashed out of the water
onto the river bank.

20

21

TEACH ON

Anak climbed a tree and dangled the chicken just above the crocodile.
With one gulp, the crocodile swallowed the chicken whole.
The poison worked quickly.
The crocodile twitched, then crashed to the ground.
Dead!

Anak climbed down the tree.
"Quick! Quick!" he called.

Everyone came running. They saw the crocodile. They looked at Anak. They couldn't believe their eyes.

"I told you I'd catch the crocodile," Anak said.

"You may not be strong, but you're clever," people said. "You are a true son of your father."

22

KIRSTY: I thought Anak might use the blowpipe and dagger — but no! The grandfather told him that there was a plant that could kill an elephant with one bite.

TEACHER: Was that a surprise for you, Kirsty?

KIRSTY: Yes! Instead of hunting the crocodile, he used the poisonous plant.

ABBIE: Well, I didn't think Anak would get the poisonous plant. I thought it would be some kind of weapon.

TEACHER: But you thought it was something other than his knife and blowpipe before, didn't you?

ABBIE: Yes, I was on the right track.

EDWARD: I got a little bit of a surprise. The pictures helped me a lot.

TEACHER: What about you, Marcus? You said that Anak put things in his bag. Were you right?

MARCUS: No. Oh . . . wait a minute. He had the rope in his bag, but not the plant.

EDWARD: Yes, he did put the leaves in his bag. It says on page 18, at the top, 'Anak plucked some of the plants and put them in his bag'.

TEACHER: So Anak *did* put something in his bag. It *was* the secret weapon, but not what you expected it to be. Let's read the last page together.

MARCUS: The secret weapon was a surprise. Everyone knows about guns and all, but not about plants like that.

DIRECTED READING-THINKING ACTIVITIES

TEACHER: Yes, that makes the setting (a place like Borneo and its jungles) especially important.

The story of how Anak caught
the crocodile was told all up and down
the river.
Everyone was happy.
Once again, they could wash clothes
and bathe their children.
Once again, they could fish.
Once again, children could play in the river.

But happiest by far was Anak the Brave,
killer of the worst crocodile in memory.

References

Hittleman, D. 1978, *Developmental Reading: A Psycholinguistic Perspective*, Rand McNally, Chicago.

Ling, Judy 1990, *Anak the Brave*, Sunshine Books, Wright Group, Seattle.

Pulvertaft, A. 1982, *Let's Breed Readers*, Ashton Scholastic, Sydney.

Stauffer, R. 1970, *The Language-Experience Approach to the Teaching of Reading*, Harper & Row, New York.

—— 1975, *Directing the Reading-Thinking Process*, Harper & Row, New York.

Weaver, C. 1979, *Reading Process and Practice: From Sociopsycholinguistics to Whole Language*, Heinemann, Portsmouth.

CHAPTER 5

HOW'S YOUR FORM?

DAVID HORNSBY AND DEBORAH SUKARNA

Features of the procedure

It helps children to distinguish between fiction and non-fiction.

It can be used with young, inexperienced readers to distinguish between fantasy and reality, and with older, experienced readers to distinguish between fiction and non-fiction texts that may not be obviously different.

Children make predictions based on language features of the title and the text and the organisation of the text.

Children may make predictions based on their knowledge of the authors and their work.

Children learn more about the language features common to fiction and non-fiction.

Children learn more about the way in which fiction and non-fiction texts are organised.

Children for whom the procedure is applicable

Children who don't consciously distinguish between fiction and non-fiction in order to set purposes for reading.

Children who need to become more aware of the different language features associated with different genres.

Experienced readers who may not be able to distinguish between non-fiction (such as in a newspaper report) and the type of fiction that is found in a well-researched historical novel.

Children who fail to make adequate use of semantic cues to direct their reading.

Children who need to adjust their writing styles to suit the various fiction and non-fiction genres.

Children who need to pay more attention to language features appropriate to the genre in which they are writing.

Size of group

This is most appropriate with small groups. However, it could be taught to a whole class when the focus is upon learning the procedure itself rather than the language skills and strategies that it helps to develop.

Materials and preparation

For younger children, or for children who have not been required to consider genre before, choose two reasonably short books that are clearly fiction and non-fiction; for example, *The Very Hungry Caterpillar* (Eric Carle) and *Caterpillar Diary* (David Drew).

For experienced readers, choose two texts where the differences between fiction and non-fiction are subtle; for example, a factual book about dolphins and an extract from the novel *Island of the Blue Dolphins* (Scott O'Dell).

The teacher must know the books or read them beforehand, and in order to question the children effectively will need to note differences in language features, format, organisation and so on, as shown below.

Language features
* specific participants or generalised participants
* imaginative description or realistic description
* direct speech
* formal or informal language
* use of personal pronouns or impersonal pronouns
* technical or specialised vocabulary

Language style
* personal feelings or factual statements
* use of humour

Organisation
* front-cover differences
* title pages, contents pages, indexes, glossaries
* chapter-heading differences
* use of headings and subheadings
* use of illustrations
* use of diagrams, graphs, photographs, labels
* use of footnotes

Procedure

Teacher action

Teacher selects a fiction book and a non-fiction book that have a common topic; for example, a selection from *Island of the Blue Dolphins* and a non-fiction book about dolphins.

Teacher writes the two titles on the chalkboard and asks, 'What do you think these books will be about? How will they be the same? How will they be different? How do you know?'.

Teacher displays the front covers of the books and asks, 'What extra clues do we get now about how the books will be similar and how they will be different?'.

If necessary, teacher draws attention to the names of the authors and asks, 'Do you know these authors? If you know any of their other work, how does this influence your predictions?'.

Teacher reads the first page of each book (or two pages if the first has only a line or two of text).

Pupil action

Children predict what they think the books will be about and give reasons for their possible similarities and differences.

Children respond from the extra clues (illustrations, cover design, author's name or equivalent, logos and so on).

Children use the knowledge they have about the authors and their work to modify or add to their predictions.

Children discuss similarities and differences.

Teacher action	*Pupil action*
Teacher finishes reading the books (or relevant extracts if the books are too long) without showing them. The purpose here is for the children to focus upon oral language cues that will help them determine whether the text is fiction or non-fiction.	Children listen for cues to help them determine whether the titles are fiction or non-fiction (e.g. use of formal or informal language, language style, language structures such as direct speech, listing, technical or specialised vocabulary and so on).
Teacher asks in what ways the two pieces of writing are similar. How did the authors write about the common subject? What purposes did the authors have? If authors write fiction, how do they use language? If authors write non-fiction, how do they use language?	Children discuss these questions in pairs. They refer to the texts in their discussion.
Teacher now asks about features such as layout, use of table of contents or index, illustrations, diagrams and so on.	Children discuss the similarities and differences between these features of the two books.
Bringing the whole group together, teacher asks, 'What have we learned about the differences between fiction and non-fiction?', encouraging generalisations that refer to all texts, not just the two used.	Children recall the similarities and differences they discussed and share them with the whole group, referring to examples from the two texts to illustrate the points; they may refer to other texts to make generalisations.
Teacher summarises findings on a chart or on the chalkboard.	

Other applications

Compare your form

Working in pairs, the children are asked to select a topic (for example, 'weather' or 'cars' or 'magic'). They then use the school library to locate both a non-fiction reference (a book, a pamphlet, an encyclopaedia entry) and a piece of fiction (a picture book, a poem, an extract from a novel) about the topic. They list the different ways in which the authors have written about it and prepare to share them with the class or a group.

Change your form

Children take a favourite picture book (such as *Don't Forget the Bacon* by Pat Hutchins) or a well-known fable (such as 'The Lion and the Mouse') and rewrite the narrative in a non-fiction form; for instance, as a newspaper report, a procedure, an interview or an explanation.

Is that a fact?

Children are supplied with an informational narrative text, such as *The Message of the Dance* (Ann Coleridge). Working in pairs, they read the text carefully and note on a chart which parts are factual and which fictional.

Message of the Dance	
Fact	*Fiction*
Nursing bees bring pollen and honey to the grubs.	The bee has a name — Lizzie.
	Bees dream.
After several days of eating pollen and honey, the grubs 'sleep' and begin their change.	Bees talk.
	The inside of the grub becomes 'grub soup'.
The grubs' shape changes and they become pupae.	

Children compare charts and justify or change what they have written by referring to the text. If necessary, other non-fiction references may be consulted. Each pair then share their work with the class.

If appropriate, the information on the charts could be used as a springboard for written reports.

References

Carle, Eric 1974, *The Very Hungry Caterpillar*, Puffin, Harmondsworth.

Coleridge, Anne 1989, *The Message of the Dance*, Language Works, Modern Curriculum Press, Cleveland, Ohio.

Derewianka, Beverly 1990, *Exploring How Texts Work*, Primary English Teaching Association, Rozelle, NSW.

Drew, David 1987, *Caterpillar Diary*, Informazing, Rigby Education, Crystal Lake, Illinois.

Goodman, Yetta & Burke, Carolyn 1980, *Reading Strategies: Focus on Comprehension*, Holt, Rinehart & Winston, New York.

Hutchins, Pat 1978, *Don't Forget the Bacon*, Puffin, Harmondsworth.

O'Dell, Scott 1960, *Island of the Blue Dolphins*, Houghton Mifflin, Boston, Mass.

WingJan, Lesley 1991, *Write Ways: Modelling Writing Forms*, Oxford University Press, Melbourne.

CHAPTER 6

POSSIBLE SENTENCES

DEBORAH SUKARNA

Features of the procedure

Prediction

The main feature of this procedure is the requirement that children use their broad knowledge of a subject to predict how given words might be used in factual text supplied. They write sentences that might possibly be found in the text.

Confirmation

Children have opportunities to read the original text and to confirm or reject their possible sentences in the light of that text.

Setting purposes

The procedure assists children to set purposes for their reading and writing. They know what they are to do and why they are doing it.

Use of personal knowledge

The fact that children are required to use and express personal knowledge means that they are more likely to be engaged in the procedure.

Integration of listening/speaking/reading/writing/thinking

The procedure requires children to interact and share, using all modes of language. It encourages them to present their ideas to each other, to justify them, to listen to others' points of view and consequently to evaluate their own work.

Children for whom this procedure is applicable

All readers and writers, as it helps with many reading/writing strategies.

Reluctant writers of non-fiction who need to develop confidence.

Children who have difficulty writing ideas logically and in sequence.

Writers who need to learn the language features of non-fiction text.

Readers who need to be immersed in more non-fiction.

Readers who need to be more conscious of the role of prediction in reading.

Readers who fail to use their non-visual information (current 'head' knowledge and experience) to interpret the visual information (text) in front of them.

Size of group

This procedure is best conducted with small, mixed-ability groups of about eight to ten. They ought to be paired so that a less capable child works with a more capable one.

It is also possible to teach the whole class the procedure if they work in pairs. However, once they understand it, to work in groups is more productive.

Materials and preparation

Short selections of non-fiction material are required, each one containing several key words that can be used for prediction purposes. Since prediction is a key strategy the material should be unknown to the children, but written in a familiar genre. Some of the key words used should be easy (familiar), some significant for providing information on the topic, and a few challenging (unlikely to be known).

Multiple copies of the text would be available so that each child can have one. However, it is often appropriate to use a selection from a longer non-fiction book; in this case, the teacher would make copies of the selection or use an overhead projector.

Procedure

This procedure is based on a short non-fiction text, *The Life of the Butterfly*.

Teacher action

Teacher displays and reads the title of the book, asking questions such as 'What kind of book or article would have a title like this?', 'What information would you expect to find in it?'.

Teacher displays the key words as a list and reads through them, not giving any meanings at this stage.

Teacher says, 'These are key words taken from *The Life of the Butterfly*. Use them to write sentences that provide information you might find in the book. You must use **all** the key words'. Teacher points out that more than one key word may be used in a single sentence and that the sentences need not be connected.

Pupil action

Children cue into the form of the text (e.g. report, description, instructions or procedure). They listen to one another and also ask questions or make comments.

Children follow the listed words as the teacher reads.

Children write their 'possible sentences'. They predict *possible* meanings of any words they do not know and include those words in their sentences.

eggs	caterpillar	hatch	pupa
butterfly	feelers	proboscis	

> A butterfly lays its eggs on a leaf.
> Little caterpillars hatch from the eggs.
> A caterpillar changes into a pupa.
> A new butterfly has feelers to feel with and a proboscis to protect it.

Teacher action	Pupil action
Teachers asks volunteers to read their possible sentences to the class.	Children receive the volunteers' sentences uncritically.
Teacher distributes a copy of the book to each child.	Children read text silently or watch and listen as teacher reads it aloud, according to the match between the text and the children's reading ability.
Teacher asks children to work in pairs and to (a) read their sentences to each other and (b) find sentences that are confirmed by the text.	Children read the text, then confirm, modify or reject their sentences. They discuss any additional information that they have provided.
Teacher asks pairs to volunteer to share their findings with the whole group.	Children explain why sentences were confirmed, rejected or modified.
Teacher leads general group discussion.	

If the purpose was to have students read the text and gain information, the activity ends here. However, the procedure can continue (see 'Other applications').

Eggs are laid by the butterfly.
Caterpillars hatch and eat the leaves.
The pupa is a grown-up caterpillar
and it changes into a butterfly.
Butterflies can sense things with their
feelers. Butterflies need their
proboscis to probe the air.

POSSIBLE SENTENCES

49

Other applications

Report writing

The sentences that were confirmed by the text can now be used as the basis of a report on the subject. Additional research will probably be necessary, but the 'possible sentences' provide a starting point in the child's own words. There is now less chance that text from reference books will simply be regurgitated.

Oral possible sentences

The procedure can be done orally with younger readers or with less capable older readers; the teacher acts as scribe and writes the sentences on the chalkboard. The whole group works together, so six to eight would be the optimal number. This is also an excellent procedure with children for whom English is a second language.

Drawing possible sentences

While the children are writing their possible sentences, they are also encouraged to use illustrations to further demonstrate their understandings. The illustrations are discussed along with the sentences. This alternative is relevant for children of all ages.

Possible sentences and evaluation

Using language to process information
As children discuss their possible sentences, teachers listen to their interactions and gain valuable information about how they use language to learn and how they process text — their reading and writing skills, strategies and behaviours.

Content
The procedure can be used at the beginning of a unit of work to evaluate what the children already know about the subject area and at the end of a unit to evaluate what has been learned.

Classroom examples

One teacher used the Sunshine book *Dinosaurs* with six children from her Year 2 class at the beginning of the school year. Five of the children were six years old; one had just turned seven. The teacher adapted the procedure for children of this age.

Day 1

The title and the key words were written on the chalkboard.

In view of their age, the children were asked to write sentences only for as many of the words as they could understand. They were given coloured cardboard for their sentences and were also asked to use illustrations to help show their meanings.

Day 2

The teacher met with the six children so that they could share their sentences and illustrations.

Mike wrote, 'Dinosaurs laid eggs long long ago'.

His illustration and discussion showed he knew that some dinosaurs flew, some walked on two legs and some on four legs, that dinosaurs came in different shapes and sizes and that they hatched out of eggs.

Andrew wrote, 'Dinosaurs were extinct for many many years'. The teacher knew what Andrew meant, but asked him if dinosaurs were *still* extinct. She helped him to express what he meant — that they have been extinct for many many years and always will be. Later, he wrote: 'If something is extinct it won't come alive'.

References

Australian Capital Territory Schools Authority (n.d.), *Reading/Writing — Developing Literacy*, Canberra Literacy Program, unit 2.

Drew, David 1989, *The Life of the Butterfly*, Informazing, Rigby Education, Crystal Lake, Illinois.

Johnson, Terry 1984, Presentation on possible sentences at Australian Reading Association National Conference, Brisbane.

Cutting, Brian & Cutting, Jillian 1988, *Dinosaurs*, Sunshine Books, Wright Group, Seattle.

CHAPTER 7

RHYME READING

MARY McDONALD

Features of rhyme reading

An extended procedure

This procedure cannot be completed in one teaching session; it will more often take four or five. For the example outlined below a four-session cycle is suggested.

A versatile procedure

Teachers may select rhymes for a variety of purposes: to complement a unit of work, to focus upon a particular language structure, to encourage use of a particular reading strategy or to develop a sense of 'community enjoyment'. Once the basic procedure is in practice, it can be adapted in many ways to suit teachers' purposes.

Active participation

The rhymes are chosen to provide genuine enjoyment either through subject matter or rhythmic patterns, or both.

In-built success

The activities are structured in such a way that success is ensured at all stages of the procedure. This enhances the children's self-esteem and maintains their interest.

Independence

The procedure can stand alone. It does not have to depend upon 'work in progress' in the language arts program. Once a rhyme is chosen, it can provide sufficient content for the procedure.

Children for whom rhyme reading is applicable

Children from non-English-speaking backgrounds.

Young children who are beginning to learn to read.

Non-confident readers at any level in the school.

Children who need practice with fluent and expressive oral reading.

Children who need to build up a basic sight vocabulary, using context.

Children who are 'turned off' reading.

Children who overemphasise one reading strategy at the expense of others, since the procedure requires that all reading strategies are used interdependently.

Children who benefit from mime, movement and forms of expression other than language.

Size of group

Rhyme reading is best conducted with groups of eight to ten children. The initial presentation of the rhyme and the enjoyment of it may involve the whole class; however, teaching points arising from the reading will be done with small groups, which come together as the teacher realises their common need.

Materials and preparation

Rhymes often appeal because of their rhythm; however, the content also should be appealing. Teachers should consider children's ages and interests when choosing rhymes, and it is important that they are able to be memorised quickly and easily; the meaning in some is obscure, and this can hinder memorisation.

Children who are just learning English or are struggling with the language should be given the opportunity of learning the procedure with rhymes from their own culture. If a bilingual teacher or parent is available, the rhyme could be presented first in the child's own language.

When the procedure is first used, the rhymes should be simple and short or else already well-known orally (for example, playground rhymes or chants). Longer and more complex rhymes can be used as the children become familiar with the procedure and develop their reading skills.

Three large copies of the rhyme are made:

copy 1 for the group to use during the introductory activity;

copy 2 to be cut up as sentence strips (or 'lines' from the rhyme);

copy 3 to be cut up into word cards for matching, sequencing and games.

Each child also receives a small copy of the rhyme. This can be saved and pasted into a 'Rhyme Book', which can be very useful for sharing with others (including parents) and for revisiting earlier rhymes for rereading and further enjoyment. The Rhyme Book can also become a substantial record of what the child is able to read independently, a source of pride and a cause for celebration.

The teacher will need to plan and prepare activities for independent work related to the rhyme — generally three activities that provide different opportunities for skill development, often including:

* a sequencing activity;
* a cloze activity;
* a word-recognition activity.

Further activities will provide for artistic, dramatic or musical expression as support for reading.

Procedure

The following procedure is written for four sessions over four days. However, the sessions could be covered in three, four or five days, depending upon the teacher's work plan.

There is a daily routine:

* introductory activity
* teaching activity
* independent activity

An activity can be done independently only *after* the children know the rhyme and have worked through similar activities with the teacher.

Day 1

Introduction

Children learn the rhyme orally (if it is not already known). Print is not necessarily used at this stage; the rhyme is learned by heart. Activities to assist during reciting could include:

* clapping on the beat;
* saying one line each;
* performing hand and body actions to go with the rhyme.

Teaching activity

A large copy of the rhyme is displayed and the teacher reads through it several times, running a finger under each word as it is read. Even if the children know the rhyme, this step should not be missed; it is important for them to match what they may already know (aurally) with the print.

* Focus: directionality and one-to-one matching of the spoken word with the written word.
* Participation: some children may volunteer at this stage to point to the words as the group is involved in choral reading.

Independent activity

Children are given individual copies of the rhyme to place in Rhyme Books and illustrate. The teacher reads through the rhyme with each child as other group members are illustrating.

Day 2

Introductory activity

Children chant and enjoy the rhyme, then read it and focus on matching spoken word with printed words; it is next reread with different groups taking different parts (for example, pairs or trios reading alternate lines). Only when the rhyme is well-known orally should the next activity be undertaken.

Teaching activity

Line-sequencing strips (made from copy 2) are introduced and children invited to match the strips to the whole text (copy 1). All the strips are provided and the children put them down in sequence. Strips are jumbled and the process repeated as appropriate.

Independent activity

Children are given individual copies of the jumbled rhyme; they cut out the lines and paste them down in the correct order. They may refer to their own copies or, if necessary, to the large copy on display. On completion, children read the rhyme aloud, indicating the words with their fingers as they read them.

Day 3

Introductory activity

Children chant and enjoy the rhyme. It is reread if necessary, focusing on matching spoken word with printed word. Individual children may wish to read it for their groups. Games can be played (for example, the teacher nominates a word and children clap when the word is read).

Teaching activity

This is a cloze activity aimed at identifying individual words. Children close their eyes while the teacher covers two, three or more words, according to difficulty of text.

The group read the text together, supplying the missing words. (This should be possible. Since the group knows the rhyme orally, success is ensured.) The words are then uncovered, to be checked. This is repeated several times, with individual volunteers. The teacher affirms children's positive responses.

Independent activity

This can be an art/craft activity related to the rhyme, or a music or dramatic activity appropriate to it.

Day 4

Introduction

Children chant and enjoy the rhyme, reread it, and play oral cloze games and sequencing games.

Teaching activity

Common letters or letter clusters are chosen and the words containing them covered. As children read the text together, they predict the covered words. When a prediction is made, the teacher uncovers the words and asks the children if that graphic information confirms their prediction. Individual word cards (from copy 3 of text) are used to have children classify words according to letter or cluster. (At this stage it is most useful to focus upon initial letters or letter clusters, as they provide more information for prediction in reading.)

Independent activity

For an individual written cloze activity, children are given copies of the rhyme with some words deleted (no more more than one word per line at this stage). Misspellings are not penalised.

Other applications

Teachers may select rhymes that complement content being studied in current units of work. For example, if an integrated unit on 'Recreation' is underway, it would be appropriate to select playground rhymes (including the many skipping rhymes).

A student Rhyme Book has been mentioned in the procedure outlined above. This is developed over time as the procedure is repeated with different rhymes and becomes a useful resource for further activities.

Once the rhyme is well known and can be read independently, the teacher can use it as text for:

* cloze with medial and final letters or letter clusters omitted;
* letter searches and sound searches (see chapter 8);
* identifying and using rhyming words;
* cluster analysis;
* identifying parts of speech and providing synonyms;
* innovation on text;
* any appropriate artistic, musical or dramatic activities.

When children are familiar with the procedures and have experienced the independent activities many times with different rhymes, they may choose the order in which they complete the activities with new rhymes.

CHAPTER 8

SOUND AND LETTER SEARCHES

BRONWEN SCARFFE

Features of sound and letter searches

Sound and letter searches actively involve children in a close study of the complexities of standard written English.

Children learn the specific sound, rhythm and letter combinations of our language in real contexts.

Children benefit from clear explanations of how sound and letter combinations work together to form words.

Teachers have opportunities to demonstrate how readers and writers use this knowledge to construct and create meanings.

The problem-solving element of this strategy provides children with a challenge, while the analytical aspect encourages them to come to some conclusions about words and to form rules that they can independently apply when reading and writing.

Sound and letter searches integrate the teaching of spelling with the teaching of reading, writing, speaking, listening and, above all, thinking.

Their open-ended nature often compels children to pursue their searches and share their findings long after actual teaching sessions have been concluded.

Children for whom sound and letter searches are applicable

Readers and writers who have a limited knowledge of the alphabet system and how it works.

Readers and writers who are unable to isolate and identify the sounds and rhythms of language.

Readers who use the graphophonic cueing system ineffectively.

Beginning and developing readers and writers who are curious about how language works.

Readers who make nonsense miscues because of limited spelling knowledge.

Readers and writers who haven't made connections between the sounds and symbols of our language.

ESL students who need to focus upon oral language and who may need to learn English language sounds with which they are unfamiliar.

Size and nature of the group

This strategy may be employed with the whole class or with individuals, but works best with six to eight children who are able to model search and communication strategies for each other. It is also more likely that learners will make observations of desirable reading and writing behaviours in the small-group situation and will feel confident enough to take risks and 'have a go'.

The group *could* be composed of children with differing levels of understandings about written language, or a special-needs group with similar language abilities or interests.

Materials and preparation

All short fiction or non-fiction texts or excerpts that provide good models of standard written English are appropriate for sound or letter searches. They are particularly valuable when a specific sound or letter combination is evident in more than one instance.

A careful reading of texts to be used as part of the daily or weekly Literacy Program will assist teachers to identify books that will best suit their teaching purposes.

Sound searches

During a sound search the emphasis is on the oral aspect of language, so it is essential that children are actively involved in the reading or chanting of a text. The saying and hearing of words is extremely important. A written transcript of the text is not always necessary; familiarity with the sounds and rhythms of the text are more important. Songs, rhymes, poems, chants and repetitive texts are all appropriate.

Letter searches

Here the emphasis is clearly on the written aspects of language, so it is essential that all members of the group have access to a copy of the text. A class wall text, multiple copies, an overhead projector and screen or a big book will all allow for the close scrutiny of words that is essential to this strategy.

For both procedures, teachers should prepare and head charts that will allow them to record the discoveries the children are making. These may relate to specific sounds or letter combinations.

Strips of paper or card (15 cm × 15 cm) should also be cut so that younger children's conclusions, generalisations and rules can be scribed for them. More proficient readers and writers should use the strips to record their own responses to the search. They may also be used to outline or explain new strategies the children use when they are confronted with unfamiliar words in texts or when they are composing their own texts.

Display these in the class Writing Area or on the Word Wall and encourage children to add to them as their understandings grow and/or change. Use them as a starting point for further sound/letter searches or as a focus for revision.

Procedure

A general outline is given below, followed by the procedure first for a sound search and then for a letter search.

Teacher action	*Pupil action*
Focuses attention: 'We are looking for words with the ___ sound/letter combination.'	Read and engage.
Encourages interaction: 'What words did you hear/find?'.	Search and respond.
Provokes thought: 'What can you tell me about all these words?'.	Think/talk through understandings.
Generates understanding: 'What rule can you make about words with the ___ sound/letter combination?'.	Form generalisations.

Teacher action	Pupil action
Influences behaviours: 'How does this knowledge help you when you are reading and writing?'.	Relate knowledge to practice and behaviours.

Sound search

Context: small teaching group during a reading/writing workshop during the last ten-week period of the school year. Six 'special needs' kindergarten children: beginning readers who are interested in sounding words when reading and writing. *Text: Mrs Wishy Washy* — a familiar and well-loved book.

Teacher action	Pupil action
Displays cover of *Mrs Wishy Washy*.	Read title and cover details.
Asks, 'What happened at the beginning, middle and end of the story?'.	Individuals retell story, using language of text.
Begins shared reading of text.	Group takes control of the pace and expression of the reading.
Directs attention to the title. Reads it aloud, emphasising the /ee/ sound at the end of words: 'Wishy', 'Washy'.	Read the title aloud together.
Asks, 'What sound do you hear at the end of the words "Wishy" and "Washy"? Read the title with me'.	Isolate and identify the sound. Offer predictions.
Confirms responses while writing the words 'Wishy' and 'Washy' on a chart headed 'Words with the /ee/ sound'.	
Says, 'Listen for all the other words in the text that have the /ee/ sound. Read along with me'.	Reread the text together, noting words with the /ee/ sound.
Asks, 'What words did you hear?'. Lists children's samples as they are offered.	Offer discoveries.
Reads through list. 'Are there any words that don't have the /ee/ sound?'	Reread to check and confirm.
Asks, 'What can you tell me about the /ee/ sound in words?'.	Think and talk about discoveries.
Asks, 'Can we make any rules about words with the /ee/ sound?'.	Form and verbalise understandings.
Records children's names and their responses on strips.	Individuals read back their rules from strips.
Says, 'Listen for any other /ee/ sound words. Jot them down so we can add them to our chart'.	Make independent discoveries.

```
┌─────────────────────────────────────────────────────────────────┐
│  Words with the 'ee' sound                                        │
│  Wishy                        he                                  │
│  Washy                        she                                 │
│  lovely                       screamed                            │
└─────────────────────────────────────────────────────────────────┘
```

┌───┐
| **Discoveries** |
| Andrea: The /ee/ sound can come in the middle of a word. |
| Sarah: The /ee/ sound can come at the end of a word. |
| Bradley: The /ee/ sound is the same as the letter named 'E'. |
| Andrea: /Ee/ is a long sound. |
└───┘

Letter search

Context: Same special needs group, two days later. *Texts:* Multiple copies of *Mrs Wishy Washy*, the 'Words with the /ee/ sound' chart, and lap version of *Grandpa, Grandpa* (another familiar text).

Teacher action	*Pupil action*
Distributes multiple copies of *Mrs Wishy Washy*.	Read text silently.
Directs attention to /ee/ sound chart. Asks children to individually locate words with the /ee/ sound in the copies of *Mrs Wishy Washy*.	Recognise and read words in context.
Confirms efforts. Conducts group reading of list. 'Have you found any other /ee/ words to add to our list?' Adds samples with children's names.	Self-correct where necessary. Offer other samples.
Focuses attention on 'ea' letter combination. Circles the word 'screamed'. 'What two letters do you think make the /ee/ sound in the word "screamed"?' Sounds the word slowly.	Make predictions based on current understandings.
Confirms that the letters 'ea' make the /ee/ sound in the word 'screamed'.	Repeat the letter combination.
Displays copy of *Grandpa, Grandpa*. Conducts shared reading while running pointer below text.	Control pace and expression of reading. Focus attention on the written word.
Says, 'Follow the text as we read it again and clap when you hear any words with the /ee/ sound'.	Read and search.

Assists children to locate words with the /ee/ sound on each page, particularly those with the 'ea' letter combination, and adds them to chart. Conducts shared reading of list of words.

Extend understandings.

Asks, 'Which new /ee/ words on our list could be grouped with the word "screamed"? Why?'.

Offer options and explanations. Verbalise understandings.

Creates a specific list of 'ea' words, underlining the letter combination.

Asks, 'Are you aware of any other "ea" words? Where did you learn them?'. (This question aims to make children more aware of where they 'find' their words.)

Revisit learning experiences. Offer suggestions for the list of 'ea' words; become 'word watchers'.

Says, 'Let's read our rules about the /ee/ sound in words and think about rules for the "ea" letter combination. Think about how the /ee/ sound and the letter combination "ea" are connected'.

Read personal rules. Offer new generalisations. Use prior knowledge to formalise new understandings.

Words with the 'ee' sound

Wishy	me	free
Washy	we	monkey
lovely	sea	tree
he	tea	ice-cream
she	three	
screamed		

Discoveries

Andrea: The /ee/ sound can come in the middle of a word.

Sarah: The /ee/ sound can come at the end of a word.

Bradley: The /ee/ sound is the same as the name of the letter 'e'.

Andrea: The sound /ee/ is a long one.

Jason: There are lots of words with the /ee/ sound.

Sarah: Words with 'ea' can have short or long sounds.

Bradley: In some words 'e' and 'a' join together to make the /ee/ sound.

Bradley: When you see 'e' and 'a' together in a word, you know that it usually says /ee/.

Further considerations

It is essential for all beginning and developing readers and writers to be introduced to all the sounds and letter combinations of standard written English.

For some, an informal or incidental introduction will be sufficient; they will make the connections independently and will be able to apply their new knowledge readily. For most, the introduction should be well planned. Explanations should be clear and more than one experience will be essential. The timing of the teaching is crucial: sound and letter searches should be conducted when children are experimenting and trying to use reading and writing strategies that relate to particular sounds and letter combinations.

The texts being used (literature, non-fiction, children's own writing, modelled writing, environmental print, words to songs and other authentic texts) dictate the searches to be conducted; the authentic texts provide the necessary context within which they can make sense. A sequential list that dictates when isolated and random sounds and letter combinations are introduced and 'taught' is invalid and irrelevant.

Record keeping

Records of the sounds and letter combinations that individuals are able to interpret when reading and use when writing independently are helpful. They reflect children's levels of understanding and they indicate to the teacher where gaps in their learning may occur.

Record keeping should not be laborious and could indeed be done co-operatively by teacher and pupil together. Formal testing is certainly not necessary. Understandings are continually made evident in everyday reading and writing.

After introducing and teaching the procedure, it is the role of the teacher to:
* observe the children as they are reading and writing;
* jot down and analyse information about behaviours being practised;
* analyse comments and writing samples;
* plan follow-up or new sound/letter searches for individuals;
* record growth of understandings and development of new behaviours.

References

Bean, Wendy & Bouffler, Chrystine 1987, *Spell by Writing*, Primary English Teaching Association, Rozelle, NSW.
Bookshelf series, *Teacher's Resource Books*, Scholastic Inc., New York.
Butler, A. 1984, *The Storybox in the Classroom*, stage 1, Wright Group, Seattle.
Cowley, Joy 1980, *Mrs Wishy Washy*, Storybox, Level 1, Wright Group, Seattle.

CHAPTER 9

TEXT MAPPING

LESLEY WINGJAN

Features of text mapping

Improvement of the strategies that children use to organise non-fiction text as they read to learn.

Use of semantic mapping to develop text maps.

Opportunities to predict both content and structure of text.

Integration of speaking, listening, reading, writing and thinking.

Mapping, building and organising a text structure.

Encouragement of active participation in discussion.

Children for whom text mapping is applicable

Children who have difficulty reading and processing factual texts.

Children who need guidance in organising their writing.

Children who need assistance with reading for information.

Children who need to develop summarising skills.

Children who are competent readers but who need to be taken beyond a literal level of comprehension.

Size of group

Text mapping is best conducted as a small-group activity. It can be used as a whole-class activity with the children working in subgroups, but this is not as effective.

Materials and preparation

A factual text should be used, preferably related to a topic children are studying at the time.

Suitable texts may be found in some commercial reading programs, in factual trade books, in some encyclopaedia entries, in school magazines and so on. Alternatively, the teacher can compose a text related to the current topic and include the structural features of the chosen form. The text can be photocopied onto an overhead projector transparency or onto individual sheets to be used as multiple copies.

In preparing the text, all headings except the main title are erased. If it is not written in paragraphs, the teacher marks appropriate places where the children will pause and comment on the content.

Procedure

Teacher action

Teacher shows title of text and asks children to predict:
* what type of text they think the piece will be (see example 1);
* what information they think will be included.

Teacher encourages broad topic headings rather than specific information (see example 2).

Teacher lists children's predictions and encourages reasons.

Pupil action

Children sugggest possible writing genre.

Children think about possible information and suggest a general classification for each type.

Children think about content, purpose and structure of different types of text.

Example 1

Type of text
factual
fiction
explanation
report
↓

Example 2

Information expected
features
enemies
food
location
interesting facts
↓

Teacher asks children to consider their predictions and to suggest an appropriate opening (lead) sentence.

Teacher receives all responses and encourages children to justify their choice of lead sentences.

Children compose orally and share first with a partner and then with the group. They may write their lead sentences.

Children read their lead sentences and give reasons for their appropriateness.

Teacher action	Pupil action
Teacher uncovers the beginning of the text and asks children to read the lead sentence silently.	Children read the sentence, compare it with their own and discuss in pairs.
Teacher asks children to refer to earlier predictions regarding writing genre.	Children review predictions; they accept or modify them, or reject them and predict again.
Teacher writes subject of text in the centre of chalkboard, as a heading.	Alternatively, children write subject in the centre of individual sheets.
Teacher reads on and asks children to suggest a topic covering the content of the paragraph.	Children track the text as they listen, then reread quickly before suggesting possible topics.
Teacher writes possible topics around the subject heading on the chalkboard.	Children may begin copying suggested topics onto their own sheets.

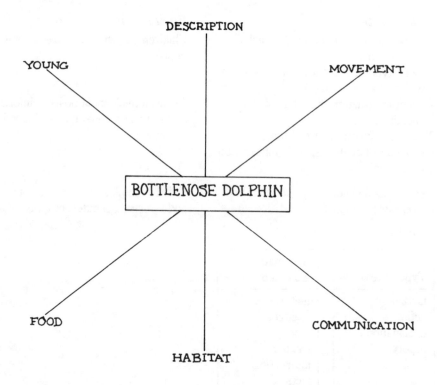

Teacher action	Pupil action
Teacher asks individual children to read aloud, paragraph by paragraph, until the complete text is read. At the end of each paragraph appropriate topics are suggested and added to the text map.	Children volunteer to read paragraphs; others follow text and suggest appropriate topics to add to the developing text map.
Teacher asks children to refer to earlier predictions and to compare them with the content of the text.	Children look for similarities and differences, the use of different words for the same meaning and so on.

Teacher action	*Pupil action*
Teacher asks children to reread text and to pause and discuss with a partner at the end of each paragraph.	Children reread and (without reading directly from the text) tell each other important facts learned from each paragraph.
Teacher supervises, observes and intervenes with individuals or groups as necessary.	Children assist each other as required and organise their reading so that they complete the task efficiently and effectively.

> This process is repeated until the complete text is read.

Concluding steps

It is important through all the final steps for the teacher to help the children articulate not only what they know about the information, but — more importantly — how the information is structured and organised.

As the process continues, children draw up their own developing text maps; this is usually best done in pairs. They add extra facts to their maps, but need to discuss the work as it progresses so that only relevant information in summarised form is recorded.

The whole group then comes together. Individuals suggest what information should be added to the chalkboard map and details are added to the 'topic lines'.

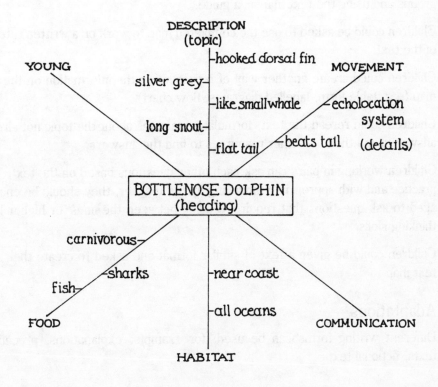

During this time the teacher has opportunities to demonstrate how information might be organised, and both teacher and children should refer to the text to relocate and check information.

The teacher discusses ways in which the information was organised and may ask:
* what the purpose of the text was;
* how the information was arranged;
* what the author needed to know to write the text;
* what the children had to know to understand the text.

It may be appropriate at this stage to focus on the features that lead the children to identify the text as a particular genre. However, it is quite possible that they will have identified the genre at an early stage, and that will be celebrated.

If appropriate, the teacher may require the children to write in their Learning Logs, describing:
* what they have learned about the subject;
* what they have learned about the written factual text and how it is organised;
* what they found easy or difficult about this session;
* what extra help they need now.

Other applications

The teacher could ask children to create an oral retelling of the text, working in groups and using the text map as a guide.

Children could be asked to use the completed map to work on a written retelling of the text.

Children could create another way of representing the information on the text map (e.g. table form, labelled diagrams, flow chart).

Children could reread the text, formulate questions about the topic not already answered and then use other resources to find the answers.

Children working in pairs can ask each other questions based on the text. With practice and with appropriate modelling by the teacher, they should be encouraged to ask questions that require 'reading between the lines' or higher level thinking skills.

Children could be given a text of similar format and asked to create their own text map.

Adaptations

Different writing forms can be used; for example, explanations, procedural texts, fictional texts.

Big books can be used as shared texts.

The procedure can be used for children of all ages by adjusting the type and difficulty of text.

Children can use what they learn about text mapping to plan their own writing; for example, they could write the subject of their choice (the heading) and the topics (for groups of information) they would like to write about. Then, as they read to find information or use information they know, they group the key words (details) under the relevant heading.

References

Brown, H. & Cambourne, B. 1987, *Read and Retell*, Methuen, North Ryde, NSW.

Collerson, J. 1988, *Writing for Life*, Primary Teaching English Association, Rozelle, NSW.

Harste, J. & Short, K. 1988, *Creating Classrooms for Authors*, Heinemann, Portsmouth, NH.

Pigdon, K. & Woolley, M. 1984, 'Getting inside the author's head', *Towards a Reading-Writing Classroom*, Primary Teaching English Association, Rozelle, NSW.

Sloan, P. & Latham, R. 1989, *Animal Reports*, Harcourt Brace Jovanovich, Sydney.

WingJan, L. 1991, *Write Ways: Modelling Writing Forms*, Oxford University Press, Melbourne.

CHAPTER 10

TEXT TRACKING

COLLEEN HORNSBY

Features of text tracking

This is an 'assisted reading' procedure that allows the underachieving or non-confident older reader to experience success in 'continuous' or sustained reading of text.

Readers track the text and read along as they are able, while listening to the teacher or a tape recording. They continue tracking until they are confident of reading the text independently.

Success is built in to every stage, since the reader may choose to listen to the text for as long as he or she feels the need.

Repeated readings make it possible to give less attention to decoding and more to comprehension.

The procedure requires the reader to focus on large 'chunks' of text.

The procedure develops reading fluency.

Children for whom text tracking is applicable

Children who have not experienced fluent oral reading.

Children who need to become aware of what the 'flow' and style of oral reading is like.

Word-by-word readers who need to focus upon larger 'chunks' of text.

Children who continue reading ('barking at print') without attending to meaning.

Children who read without expression.

Readers for whom English is a second language and who need to experience the pitch and stress patterns of English.

Readers who have experienced failure.

Size of group

This procedure is most appropriate for use with individual children who have not responded to other instructional procedures. However, a small group (two or three only) could use a Big Book that they can all sit close to, or a group could use multiple copies at a listening post.

Materials and preparation

It is wise to start the procedure with reading material that is fairly easy, and the child should be involved in the selection of the book (or the part of a book) to be read. It is best if the text can be read in its entirety in a few minutes. Once the child knows the procedure and has read several texts more fluently texts can be increased in length, although none should take more than 10 or 15 minutes to read. Texts also should be of high interest to the child, since multiple readings are required. As the reader becomes more familiar with the procedure and more confident, the difficulty of the text can be increased as well as its length.

An audiotape will save the teacher (or parent or other helper) reading the text aloud each time it is to be reread. It also allows children to follow the procedure independently whenever they wish.

If narrative is chosen by the child, it should have a clear plot or storyline that is easy to follow.

Procedure

First session

Teacher action	*Pupil action*
Teacher sits next to child so that both can see the book. Teacher explains that they are going to read the book together and that the child should join in as much as possible.	
Teacher reads the text at normal speed (or *slightly* slower than normal) and with expression. Teacher may also run a finger along the lines to assist the child's 'tracking'.	Child follows text; at first reading may just listen and watch the teacher's moving finger, although 'reading along' is encouraged. Child comes 'in and out' of oral reading as he or she is able.

Teacher action	*Pupil action*
Teacher encourages response without asking direct questions. At this stage, any explanation required should be about *meaning*; this is not a time to focus upon decoding skills or 'bits' of language.	Child responds to text in own way. Response may be limited at this stage, but if he or she asks a question, teacher answers or explains.

Teacher rereads text, possibly slowing down slightly when the child is managing but needs more time. Rate of reading must yet be fast enough to maintain the flow of the language and the building of meaning.	Child follows again, this time participating more in the shared reading.
Teacher carefully observes child's reading behaviours and allows child to take more and more responsibility.	Child may also take over the finger tracking.
Teacher's main concern is to keep the reading going; stopping for instruction is not appropriate. (If reading is too laboured, easier text should be provided.)	Child may again respond to the reading.
Teacher provides tape.	Child plays tape and reads along with it as often as possible before the next session with teacher. Tape can be taken home for practice.

TEACH ON

Second session

Teacher rereads text after inviting child to join in.

Child reads along with teacher. Considerable improvement may already be evident.

Again teacher focuses on the style of reading and on 'keeping the reading going', lowering voice or stopping at any passage with which the child is familiar.

Child keeps reading, regardless of amount of assistance, knowing that the teacher will 'come into the reading' again when help is needed.

Teacher may provide tape again or suggest new material.

This procedure continues until the child either reads the material fluently or indicates a desire to read a different text. When he or she is confident with the material, opportunities should be provided for oral reading to others.

Reference

Morgan, Roger 1986, *Helping Children Read: The Paired Reading Handbook*, Methuen, London.

There are no specific reference works on text tracking. The process has evolved from others, such as assisted reading, Neurological Impress Method and repeated readings.

Read On
A Conference Approach to Reading

David Hornsby and Deborah Sukarna, with Jo-Ann Parry

Although the return to the use of 'real literature' is gaining momentum, there are still few reference books available for the teacher. This is a practical guide for implementing a reading program in classrooms. It shows how the literature strand can be organised and how an experience-based strand can be incorporated even into lesson plans featuring basal texts. The practices recommended are based on sound theory, but the emphasis of the book is on experiences and techniques developed by the authors in real situations. For those teachers interested in exploring the theoretical background, further reading lists are provided in each chapter.

Write On
A Conference Approach to Writing

Jo-Ann Parry and David Hornsby

The companion volume to the authors' *Read On* covers a number of very practical matters of concern to teachers and provides a step-by-step program for implementing a conference-based writing program. The experienced teacher of writing will find the book useful, but it should be especially valuable to teachers who want to bring writing into their classes but would appreciate some straightforward suggestions on how to proceed.